Collins
MUSIC

SECONDARY MUSIC LEADER'S HANDBOOK

INSPIRING IDEAS

**DAN FRANCIS AND
DR ELIZABETH STAFFORD**

William Collins' dream of knowledge for all began with the publication of his first book in 1819.

A self-educated mill worker, he not only enriched millions of lives, but also founded a flourishing publishing house. Today, staying true to this spirit, Collins books are packed with inspiration, innovation and practical expertise. They place you at the centre of a world of possibility and give you exactly what you need to explore it.

Published by Collins

An imprint of HarperCollins*Publishers*
The News Building, 1 London Bridge Street, London, SE1 9GF, UK

HarperCollins*Publishers*
Macken House, 39/40 Mayor Street Upper, Dublin 1, D01 C9W8, Ireland

Browse the complete Collins catalogue at **collins.co.uk**

© HarperCollins*Publishers* Limited 2025

10 9 8 7 6 5 4 3 2 1

A catalogue record for this publication is available from the British Library.

ISBN 978-0-00-875983-4

All rights reserved. No part of this publication may be reproduced, stored in a retrieval system, or transmitted in any form by any means, electronic, mechanical, photocopying, recording or otherwise, without the prior written permission of the Publisher or a licence permitting restricted copying in the United Kingdom issued by the Copyright Licensing Agency Ltd, 5th Floor, Shackleton House, 4 Battle Bridge Lane, London SE1 2HX.

Without limiting the exclusive rights of any author, contributor or the publisher of this publication, any unauthorised use of this publication to train generative artificial intelligence (AI) technologies is expressly prohibited. HarperCollins also exercise their rights under Article 4(3) of the Digital Single Market Directive 2019/790 and expressly reserve this publication from the text and data mining exception.

Authors: Dan Francis and
 Dr Elizabeth Stafford
Publisher: Tom Lydon
Proofreader: Michelle Daley
Cover images: Lemberg Vector studio/
 Shutterstock; Sergiy1975/Shutterstock
Cover design: Fresh Lemon Australia
Internal design: Fresh Lemon Australia
Production controller: Bethany Brohm
Printed and bound by: Ashford Colour Ltd

MIX
Paper | Supporting responsible forestry
FSC™ C007454

This book contains FSC™ certified paper and other controlled sources to ensure responsible forest management.

For more information visit: www.harpercollins.co.uk/green

collins.co.uk/sustainability

Acknowledgements

The publishers gratefully acknowledge the permission granted to reproduce the copyright material in this book. Every effort has been made to trace copyright holders and to obtain their permission for the use of copyright material. The publishers will gladly receive any information enabling them to rectify any error or omission at the first opportunity.

Dan Francis: To my wife, Marie, the greatest cheerleader for music education I've ever met; my constant support and fact-checker. To my three children, who have given me more than I ever thought possible. To my own teachers and mentors, Kevin Stannard, Mike Skitt, Richard Hallam, Cathy Roberts and the late Anna Haxworth, who taught me what great teaching was all about. And to the many others I've engaged with who have inspired me to reflect on what students need from the people who are shaping their world.

Dr Elizabeth Stafford: To my flautist niece Natasha, pianist nephew Jack, nephew Harry who is yet to find his instrument, and niece Isabella who was born at the same time as this book. Thank you for inspiring me every day to try to make music education better for wonderful young people just like you!

Contents

Introduction	5
Chapter 1: Preparing for the role	**6**
What is the role of head of music?	6
What skills and knowledge do you need?	8
Capacity builders, barriers and managing your own time	11
Chapter 2: Designing your curriculum – practical considerations	**12**
Getting started	12
Designing a curriculum from scratch	14
Chapter 3: Designing your curriculum – musical skills and knowledge	**18**
The curriculum planning challenge	18
Skills and knowledge	20
Progress and progression	24
Ofsted curriculum pillars	26
Notation and visual aids	31
Chapter 4: Designing your curriculum – assessment and tracking	**34**
The purpose of assessment	34
Managing your assessment data and tracking progress	37
Chapter 5: Supporting your colleagues with music	**44**
Supporting the specialists within your department	44
Supporting non-specialists	48
Chapter 6: Defining your co-curricular programme	**53**
Defining the purpose of your co-curricular and instrumental programme	53
Audit your offer	54
Instrumental tuition	57
Monitoring, measuring and managing quality and impact	60
Celebrating your co-curricular programme	61

Chapter 7: Preparing for the role   **63**

Teaching rooms   63
Practice rooms   65
Instruments   65
Music technology   69
Print and digital media   72
Copyright and licensing   73
Finances and resource management   74

Chapter 8: Creating a music development plan   **76**

What is a development plan?   76
Defining your vision: Where do you want to be?   76
Auditing your provision: Where are you now?   77
Creating the detail: How do you get there?   78
Aligning with the school improvement plan   79
Aligning with non-statutory guidance   80

Conclusion   **80**

Introduction

Congratulations! You have been appointed as music subject leader. Perhaps you are heading up a big department with many teachers; perhaps you are the default head of a department of one. Maybe you have been in the role for a while and are looking for some inspiration, or this could be a brand-new role and you are wondering how to get started. Whatever your situation, this handbook has been written to support you in this challenging but rewarding position.

This handbook will support you to develop all aspects of music in your school, whatever your starting point. It will help you to analyse and audit your current music provision in order to identify areas for improvement, and it will help you to create a development plan to address these. It will support you in your interactions with the Senior Leadership Team (SLT) and other teaching colleagues, whether they are specialists or non-specialists. It will show you how to create a curriculum and a co-curricular programme that meet the needs of your students and encourage them to progress and excel in music. This book covers a multitude of issues and skills. You can read it cover to cover or dip in and out.

The role of music subject leader should be a pleasure, not a chore. We hope that this book will help enhance your experience of this role, giving you the confidence, knowledge and skills to truly enjoy leading music in your school.

Chapter 1

Preparing for the role

In this chapter you will get an overview of what your role involves and what it doesn't involve. It will help you to focus your efforts where they will best serve your students and the wider school, making you an effective subject leader.

What is the role of head of music?

As subject leader/head of department for music, you are the person who decides how to achieve the best musical outcomes for your students. Your main responsibility will be to design and deliver a curriculum that gives students the knowledge they need to make progress against their targets. You will also need to ensure that you offer the right sort of activities outside the classroom – provision that will enhance student learning and promote the school. Finally, you will need to make a plan to use the resources you have in the time you have available so that you can sustain and build your department over time.

Meeting targets

Schools are data-rich environments and every student in your classroom will have been assigned their own target, which will have been determined from a range of data points that sit outside the music department. They will also be part of a cohort of students, whose progress and achievement the school will be monitoring as a group. In fact, they could be part of any number of cohorts based on their:
- age and birthday
- gender
- ethnicity
- socio-economic status

- prior attainment at primary school
- special educational or additional needs.

You will have access to this information and be required to feed back on their development to your line manager as well as ensuring that anyone working in your department is aware of any whole-school strategies that are in place to support them.

As these targets assigned to your students are not based on any musical information, it can be tempting to feel that they are not relevant or accurate. Student A may have achieved a really high Key Stage 2 result, but they don't play a musical instrument. How can they possibly achieve the same high target as the amazing guitarist you have in the same year group? Given that Student B is such a great singer, is there really any point taking note of the low target they have due to their low cognitive abilities test (CAT) score?

In fact, these targets are useful in identifying students:
- who have particularly good potential to acquire academic knowledge
- who will need particular support with certain areas of the curriculum
- whose musical performance skills may be masking weaknesses elsewhere
- who would benefit from additional opportunities that they are unable to access elsewhere.

The targets can, then, be a really useful tool to help with the strategic development of your department and in gaining support from the wider school community for particular interventions.

Setting targets

You may find that you have responsibility for managing other colleagues, in which case you will want them to feed into the vision you have for your department. If they are an employed colleague, you will need to agree some targets for which you will share responsibility. The targets you set will need to feed into wider whole-school targets and have a focus on developing your department, your colleagues and your students. Writing a department development plan that has short- (this year), medium- (two- to three-year) and long-term (three- to five-year) goals will help you to shape what these targets should be.

If you need to set a target for someone who is not directly employed by your school, such as a visiting instrumental teacher or a workshop leader, you will want to have a clear idea of how they can support your department goals and you should liaise with them to ensure they are able to achieve that outcome.

Chapter 1: Preparing for the role

What skills and knowledge do you need?

As subject leader, you will need to both lead and manage the department.

Leadership skills

Set out your strategic vision for the department based on an audit of:

- the engagement and achievement of the students
- 'whole school' priorities
- what will make your department uniquely attractive
- resources
- staffing.

Next, establish a timeline that sets out the steps you will need to take to get there.

You will need to identify which stakeholders need to share in this vision and how you will best communicate it to them:

- **SLT:** The focus of the SLT may well be on the school finances; academic standards; the school's reputation; and reporting to governors, Ofsted and other stakeholders. They may have a limited lived experience of music and will be busy. They will also have been a head of department previously, will be focussed on supporting the students in the school's care, and will be mindful of everyone's mental health and wellbeing.

- **Parents or carers:** Inevitably, parents or carers will focus on the needs of their own child and on how much capacity they have to support them in terms of both time and finances. They may have a limited lived experience of music and their own philosophy and motivations may or may not align with those of the school. They will be concerned with either their child's emotional or academic development, or both, and may have a particular view on the type of musical achievement and progress they want for their child.

- **External providers:** Your department may represent a small amount of their overall time. They may have a limited lived experience of music and a set model of delivery. They will also be concerned with finances and may have a focus on short-term musical engagement rather than a long-term strategic view.

- **Students:** Your students may not need to know what your vision for the department is. Instead, you will need to design your vision so that they can perceive the positive impact it has on their lessons, the opportunities they can access outside lessons and how music looks and feels within the classroom and across the school.

As subject leader, you will want to be a professional presence, demonstrating the behaviours you want to see in your students and making sure you keep other colleagues informed of how musical activity is supporting students across the school.

Management skills

As subject leader, you will be managing a range of conflicting priorities, from reacting to matters arising with students in your own lessons through to proactively planning new long-term projects.

Use your department development plan as a management tool, making sure that any planned activity supports one of the goals within it. Refer back to it to make sure that the timeline you have set remains realistic and/or that you are sticking to it.

Use the school calendar as a management tool, making sure everyone is working towards clear department assessment deadlines, whole-school events and department concerts, events and visits. Make sure you are clear on what responsibilities other staff have in supporting these events and that students are also clear about what is happening.

Use data as a management tool, making sure your team is accessing it when discussing things with parents or carers; when reflecting on lesson planning; when discussing the progress of particular cohorts; and when reviewing and planning additional activities and interventions.

Make sure you understand the financial position of your department, drawing on support from the finance department to break down what percentage is spent on different areas. Where resource is a barrier to supporting student progress, make sure you can access data to highlight where and how additional resource will positively impact on whole-school priorities.

Knowledge

You will already be a good teacher and a good musician. You will still need to build knowledge of:

- musical styles and genres that are outside your own lived experience
- how to use existing and emerging technologies
- policies and research in music education
- opportunities in the wider community that can support your students
- the existing make-up of the students in your school
- the skills and experience of the staff working in your department
- exam board requirements.

You do not need to be a fluent performer on the clarinet to be able to assess and develop a student's musical skill while they are performing on the clarinet. You also do not need to be a fluent producer on Logic to be able to assess and develop a student's musical skill while they are creating content. What you do need to know is what knowledge you want them to develop and how this fits into any assessment criteria set by your curriculum or the exam board.

You do not need to be the expert or leader of activities relating to every style of music ever conceived. But you do need to know how to develop students' ability to recognise how this music has been put together and help them to explore where they can engage with it further.

Top tip

It will be useful to conduct a short survey of your colleagues across all departments, SLT, instrumental tutors and support staff to find out:

- what their own instrumental learning background is
- what musical activity they engage with now, for example creating, listening, or going to gigs/concerts
- what motivates them to engage in music
- what they think makes someone a musician.

This will be helpful in identifying what their perceptions of music are and what capacity there is for you to draw on colleagues to develop music further.

Capacity builders, barriers and managing your own time

Your department will function within a school where any of the following could be a barrier or a facilitator to your department's development:

- curriculum time
- co-curricular time
- availability of staff and students
- motivation of staff and students
- school systems
- finances
- equipment
- space.

As subject leader, you will be able to work with colleagues to find ways of building capacity. This can be through:

- curriculum content
- creative collaboration
- digital access
- pastoral systems
- use of PPA (planning, preparation and assessment time)
- outcome measures.

All of these are discussed in later chapters in this book.

Top tip

Remember that you cannot do everything all at once. In order to draw on effective support from other stakeholders linked to your school community, you could follow this process:

> Identify your department vision
>
> ▼
>
> Identify what your curriculum and any wider curricula are for
>
> ▼
>
> Identify what cannot be covered with the time and resources available
>
> ▼
>
> Evaluate the most critical area to develop
>
> ▼
>
> Review your own capacity and ability to cover that area
>
> ▼
>
> Research where additional resource can come from, both in and out of school
>
> ▼
>
> Provide a clear rationale for what the additional resource will deliver – with KPIs

Chapter 1: Preparing for the role

Chapter 2

Designing your curriculum – practical considerations

In this chapter you will learn how to ensure that your curriculum meets your school's needs, whether you are designing it from scratch or revising an existing curriculum.

Getting started

> "We can often see whole KS2 and KS3 music curricula founded solely on the 'what' of lesson planning, in other words on what the children and young people will do. Much harder, but much more profitable in the long term, is to start with 'why'. 🎵
>
> Professor Martin Fautley, writing for *Primary Music Magazine*, 2019

When setting out to design or revise your existing curriculum, it is all too easy to get distracted by the exciting content that you want to include. When you start the process of curriculum planning with a list of topic ideas, in your eagerness to make all your favourite ideas fit, you run the risk of designing a curriculum that lacks coherence and which hinders progression. Instead, you should start the process of curriculum planning by considering the bigger picture: the 'why' – the reasons that you 'do' music in your school.

A great starting point for this would be to create a vision statement, perhaps based around the three Is of Intent, Implementation and Impact.

Intent
The 'big picture' of music in your school – what it is for and how it will benefit your students, including how it contributes to the school improvement plan.

Implementation
How you will achieve what you intend – what activities and resources will be available.

Impact
What students will be able to do when they leave your school – often best expressed as bullet points.

The 'intent', 'implementation' and 'impact' sandwich

Once you have established the big picture, or the *intent* of music in your school, you will be able to outline the *impact* this will have on your students. These two elements, the 'bread' of the sandwich, concern the 'why' question. Perhaps your *intent* is that all students will leave your care believing that they are 'musical' and therefore feeling able to pursue their musical interests in the future in whatever form these might take.

This might result in an *impact* of students being able to confidently talk about and analyse music, having basic skills on an instrument, and knowing how to use their singing voices. The curriculum is the *implementation* – the filling in your three Is sandwich – and it will take you from your outlined *intent* to your proposed *impact*.

It is likely that you will inherit a curriculum, so your job at this point will be to look at this and see if it will achieve your intended impact. During this process you will need to take account of why your curriculum looks the way it does. There may be additional reasons why certain instruments are always used or certain topics have been chosen, and sweeping these away to make way for your new vision might cause some upset.

Top tip

Remember that most of your students will finish their musical journey in school at the end of Year 9, so it is really important not to base your *impact* around students gaining GCSE, A Level or other musical qualifications. Your *intent* and *impact* should be for all students, not just those choosing to study music at KS4 and beyond, and that means that your KS3 curriculum needs to be full and complete in its own right and not merely a 'preparation phase' for future qualifications.

Chapter 2: Designing your curriculum – practical considerations

Designing a curriculum from scratch

Designing a curriculum from scratch will be a time-intensive, laborious, but satisfying process, as you will have full control over all the content and can be sure that it meets the outcomes that you want. You will be able to start with your own vision and to tailor all of your curriculum content and resources to deliver it, rather than having to compromise to accommodate the content already prescribed by a previous teacher.

What to include

Once you have established your vision for music, the next consideration is the 'what' – the content of your curriculum. At this point it is prudent to remember that most schools are required to follow their national curriculum. These usually require students to listen to, perform (through singing and with instruments), improvise, and compose music, and also to gain some theoretical understanding around the way music functions, its place in history, and its communication systems (for example, staff notation). Sometimes non-statutory guidelines exist, but there is no requirement to follow them, and sometimes particular content is prescribed, but more often than not it is up to subject leaders to choose the content that provides their students the opportunity to improve their musical skills.

Choosing content for your curriculum is the fun part, but it is important not to get too carried away without considering the resources that you have available (or can purchase), and the confidence and competence of your staff to teach various musical genres, styles and traditions. You may find you end up with an ambitious Plan A list of content that has to be scaled back, at least in the beginning, into something more manageable.

Top tip

When you're choosing content for your curriculum, remember to continually refer back to the 'why' question – the rationale that leads to the 'impact' section of your vision statement. It is easy to get carried away with all the amazing different topics you could cover, but if the content of your curriculum is not contributing to the aims of your overall music vision, then it needs to change.

That is OK – curriculum design is a continuous process, and over time you will be able to work towards delivering your 'curriculum of dreams'.

When considering the content of your curriculum, it is also important to consider the amount of time you have available for the teaching of music. You will need to make hard decisions about what to include, planning for 'curriculum content that might reasonably be mastered in the time available, remembering that sometimes less is more' (Ofsted, 2021).

Reflecting your school community

Another consideration when choosing content for your curriculum is the cultural make-up of your school community. Schools should reflect the communities that they serve, and this should be a consideration when including particular musical styles, genres and traditions into your curriculum.

> **Top tip**
>
> At this point you will find it useful to carry out an audit of the resources you already have in school, for example:
>
> - digital audio workstations (DAWs)
> - untuned percussion instruments
> - tuned instruments
> - sheet music and songbooks
> - backing tracks
> - CDs and videos
> - streaming subscriptions
> - speakers and sound systems
> - manuscript (staff notation) paper and whiteboards
> - music reference books.

This is not just some trendy idea to make your school look progressive, but in fact an important strategy for getting children on board with formal music education. It refers just as much to the forms of popular music that children listen to at home as it does to the musical traditions of diverse cultures. You need to remember that music is an important component of young people's sense of self-identity, and that the music that they listen to outside the classroom is likely to be much more sophisticated than the music that they can produce themselves in lessons. Ignoring children's 'own' music in your curriculum can alienate them from it.

Chapter 2: Designing your curriculum – practical considerations

"Where [classroom music activity] is not coupled in the mind of any student with the impact of actual music-making and music-taking relating to experience outside of school, the effect can be of a curriculum which resembles the scraps under a rich man's table, the cold left-overs of other people's meals, often unappetizing."

Keith Swanwick, from *Music, Mind and Education* (Routledge, 1988)

Decolonising the curriculum, and 'cultural capital'

There is a tradition across most of the Western world of prioritising Western music, particularly classical music, over and above the music from other parts of the world when teaching children about music. Historically, influential people have described classical music as the 'highest' or 'best' form of music. Government ministers in the UK in the recent past have expressed the opinion that students should be fed a diet of classical music to somehow better themselves.

In England, the concept of 'cultural capital', as interpreted by Ofsted's Inspection Framework, has unwittingly reinforced this message, as it makes the point that teachers should be introducing students to 'the best that has been thought and said' (from Ofsted's *School Inspection Handbook*, 2019). Teachers may default to Western classical music because they have been told or have assumed that it represents 'the best'. However, comparing European classical music to Indian classical music, or American pop to Indonesian gamelan music, is like comparing Dickens to Hugo, Cervantes to Shakespeare; these are not like-for-like comparisons as they use completely different languages.

Top tip

When planning for cultural capital, you will want to consider all the different musical traditions that you want your students to experience, both reflecting and broadening out from the school community, and find the 'best' examples of these to share. This will then place all the music you study on an equal footing.

Planning for learning and engagement

Another consideration when planning content for your curriculum is what Professor Martin Fautley describes as 'the difference between planning for "doing" and planning for "learning"'.

You need to ensure that the content that you select meets the learning aims, in effect moving beyond the idea that 'students are learning to play *Ode to Joy*' and reframing it as something more like: 'Students are learning how to find notes on a keyboard/play in time/play two-handed on the keyboard/read stepwise melodies from staff notation' – or whatever the actual learning intent might be. This might sound obvious, but often in music teachers default to 'learning the material' (planning for doing) as the prime purpose, rather than considering the particular musical skills that are being developed through the learning of the material (planning for learning).

You should also give careful consideration to planning for 'engagement'. This encompasses everything from considering the available resources and individual needs to considering ability levels and personal musical preferences. Lessons will not be engaging and students will make limited progress if they are sitting round waiting for their turn to use instruments or computers. Although you might be really enthusiastic about including a guitar unit, if you only have three guitars to go round a class of 30 and no prospect of buying any more by the time you teach it, this is probably best avoided!

Similarly, if you have a unit planned that you know a particular class or year group will struggle with due to additional needs or ability levels, this is the time to come up with an alternative plan that actually motivates and engages students to make progress at their own level, rather than battling through the original unit just because it is on the curriculum. It is worth bearing in mind that students' own musical preferences have a strong bearing on motivation and engagement in the classroom, so linking your units to the music that they enjoy outside lessons can provide an easy win for progress and development.

Reading recommendation

To get a good overview of the research behind successful curriculum design in music, search for Martin Fautley's article 'Curriculum Planning & Classroom Music', from *Primary Music Magazine*, issue 3.1.

Chapter 2: Designing your curriculum – practical considerations

Chapter 3

Designing your curriculum – musical skills and knowledge

In this chapter you will learn some principles of curriculum planning that will enable you and your students to focus on the different types of skills and knowledge that help them to identify as musicians.

The curriculum planning challenge

> "Music is an ongoing and incremental journey and will not look the same for all children."
>
> *The power of music to change lives: a national plan for music education*, www.gov.uk, 2022

Planning a curriculum that meets the needs of every student in your school is a constant process of reflection and evaluation, and it is highly likely that the content that worked for one year group may well need adapting for the next. Even before you consider the curriculum they will have experienced at Primary school, you need to consider how and where else they have engaged with music, and how much.

For each of these students in the table below, the curriculum you have planned represents a different fraction of the time they spend engaging with music. How they engage with different areas of your curriculum will depend on what they understand music to be, what they know about music, and, therefore, how it resonates with them as an individual.

Student 1

- Year 7 student who appears to enjoy singing in lessons and answers questions intelligently.
- Parent/carer feedback says they had whole-class brass tuition in Year 5, which they seemed to enjoy.
- Tried peripatetic flute lessons for a year but didn't really enjoy it.
- Loves listening to Taylor Swift.

Student 3

- Year 8 student who did not score well in any music assessments in Year 7, particularly in the keyboard skills project.
- Enters a talent show put on by sixth-form students and plays piano to accompany their friend who sings.
- They join the Tech Team to help with the school production and get really involved in working on the sound.

Student 2

- Year 9 student who has violin lessons and says they passed Grade 5.
- Plays in an orchestra outside school and played a solo in the school concert at Christmas.
- Didn't score very well in the latest project on the blues, where they had to write a song and improvise on the keyboard.
- Goes to the IT department after school instead of coming to the school orchestra.
- They joined the school choir but had to stop because it clashed with Maths intervention sessions.

Student 4

- Year 9 student who is in the department every lunchtime and after school playing guitar and singing their own songs.
- Performed really well in the latest band project but did not enjoy the latest composition project using technology.
- They have guitar lessons at school but say they haven't done any exams and they learn to play everything by ear and tab.
- They are teaching themselves to play the bass guitar as there's a band in Year 11 without a player.
- They want to do GCSE Music but don't like classical music.

Chapter 3: Designing your curriculum – musical skills and knowledge

As a 2012 pilot study report by Jo Saunders and Graham Welch (search for 'Communities of Music Education a Pilot Study') put it: 'Formal and non-formal musical provision may exist as musical pathways that run in parallel or opposing pathways, with little or no overlap. ... [There can be a] perceived mismatch between the academic (written) approach in formal settings and the practical (music-making) approach in non-formal settings... Pupil–teacher relationships have been found to be more positive where pupils feel that they are able to achieve ... [and where the relationship is] respectful of, and interested in, the young person's musical opinions and preferences.'

A curriculum will be most effective if it has a tight focus on the skills and knowledge you want students to develop and if it:

1. builds on pre-existing skills and experience learnt outside the classroom
2. teaches new skills and knowledge.

Skills and knowledge

"Learning is defined as an alteration in long-term memory. If nothing has altered in long-term memory, nothing has been learned."

Sweller, Ayres and Kalyuga, *Cognitive Load Theory*, 2011

Students can often be highly engaged in a musical activity but may simply be drawing on a pre-existing set of skills to produce more of the same. A successful curriculum will help the student to identify what these skills are and how they are using them to make the music they are producing. In order to do this, it's helpful to look at each aspect of your planned content and identify whether it is developing your students':

- knowledge **of** music
- knowledge about **how to** make music
- knowledge **about** music.

Tacit, substantive and disciplinary knowledge

Planned content can also be thought about in terms of different realms of knowledge:

- **Tacit knowledge:** Knowledge that students pick up through everyday engagement with music

- **Substantive/declarative knowledge:** The elements, ingredients and things that are used to make music. These are the skills and knowledge you will teach through your curriculum
- **Disciplinary/procedural knowledge:** Knowing how musicians use the things they know to create music.

Ofsted's *Music Subject Report* (Sept 2023) refers to both declarative and procedural knowledge but does not refer to tacit knowledge, and this is quite helpful for planning purposes. The declarative and procedural knowledge you intend students to develop and demonstrate should be explicitly written into your curriculum plan. The tacit knowledge students already possess should be used implicitly to inform what you need to teach and what sort of differentiation you need to build in to each lesson for different cohorts.

Threshold concepts

The term 'threshold concepts' commonly refers to concepts that change the way a student thinks about a topic, without which they wouldn't have been able to properly understand it.

Within music, it is useful to think of these as the key musical concepts that students need to understand in order to be able to move on to the next phase of their learning.

In the 'Building your band' example on the following pages, the substantive knowledge is focussed on developing students' ability to:

- construct a basic chord
- read a standard chord chart and relate this to standard chord sequences that are put together within standard pop structures
- understand the role their instrument plays in affecting the texture in a pop song.

The disciplinary knowledge is focussed on:

- identifying the key aspects of performing their instrument with increasing control within a group.

The threshold concepts are linked to:

- performing skills
- music theory
- conventions in music.

Identifying the musical skills and knowledge in this way should help you, your team and your students to focus on the development you want to see rather than simply completing an activity where it can be hard to identify what progress they have made. More of this in Chapter 4

Key Stage 3

Year 8 – Spring term

Building your band

Aims	• Develop the ability to perform a range of songs on different instruments with others • Develop an understanding of the standard chord progressions found in pop songs • Recognise major-scale chords I, ii, iii, IV, V, and vi (and why they are written like this) • Develop a working knowledge of lead sheets and chord charts • Develop an understanding of verse-chorus structure • Develop an understanding of instrumentation in pop songs and the roles of each instrument
Disciplinary knowledge	**Ability to perform in time with others on at least one instrument:** • Internal pulse at different tempos • Reaction and interaction with others • Play single notes or full chords of I, ii, iii, IV and V on bass, piano or guitar • Smooth movement between chords and sections of songs • Rhythmic variation of chord notes using articulation • Use of dynamics and balance **Ability to apply knowledge of chords:** • Record a four-bar chord sequence in time to a click track • Select chord notes to voice/assign to bass, melody line, backing vocals, horns, etc • Create three tracks on Logic or as a band: a melody track, accompaniment track, and a bass track

Key Stage 3	
Year 8 – Spring term	
Building your band	

Substantive knowledge	**Ability to understand and explain:**
	• Single-note bass guitar and guitar tab
	• How to build chords on the keyboard using root, 3rd and 5th
	• Chords based on the major scale as Roman numerals (I, ii, iii, IV, V, vi)
	• Four-bar chord sequences as written on chord charts
	• 12-bar blues, 32-bar song form and verse-chorus structure
	• Texture in terms of bassline, chords, accompaniment, lead
	• Standard instruments used in pop songs
	   - Backline: drums, bass, keys, rhythm guitar
	   - Frontline: vocals, lead guitar, sax, trumpet, trombone, BVox (backing vocals)

Threshold concepts	• Strings on the guitar/bass and link to tab reading • You can play in all keys on the piano keyboard, and the link to building chords • Chords in relation to a tonal centre (I, V, ii, and IV) • Four-bar phrases

Progress and progression

Progress can be defined as how much a student has developed their musical skills and knowledge over a set period of time.

Progression can be defined as their movement from one term to the next, or from one type of musical activity to the next.

Progression

Tracking progression is a useful measure of engagement and is helpful to consider when planning your curriculum.

At secondary level, it is useful to think of your curriculum as building on the learning that takes place outside the classroom, including through any instrumental exams. It can be useful to think of it as reverse engineering the tacit knowledge students already have and then building out and around it.

Top tip

Bear in mind that the instrumental grade system is based on progression from one grade to the next, developing students' ability to become increasingly specialised on their chosen instrument. Grades 1 to 3 are at Level 1 on the Regulated Qualifications Framework (RQF) in the UK so are at the same 'level' as 'Grades 4–1' at GCSE. However, as their progress is measured in terms of performance on an instrument, there may be other areas where their musical skills and knowledge are less well developed.

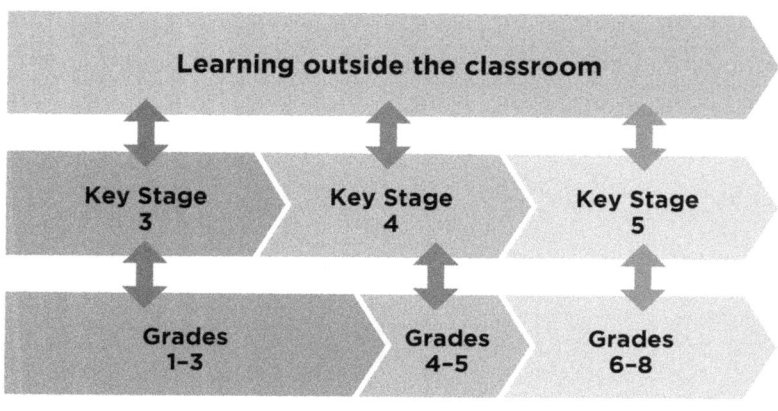

Progress

Students develop diverse realms of knowledge through different types of engagement with music, and this means that progress is rarely linear. However, it is possible to plan a curriculum that can help to solve a number of the assessment and tracking challenges that exist within music (see Chapter 4).

Thinking about threshold concepts is really useful in identifying the hierarchies that exist within musical development. For example, it is quite difficult for a student to listen to a piece of music and analyse its structure without having a working knowledge of musical phrases and cadences. It's even harder for them to compose one. However, it is perfectly possible for a student to learn how to play the melody to 'Ode to Joy' without *explicitly* thinking about each musical phrase or the chord structure underneath.

In learning how to play the melody, the student has demonstrated a really strong sense of pulse and rhythm; an ability to play the notes in the right order, maybe with some good articulation and dynamics; and either an ability to learn by ear or using some form of notation – or both.

Top tip

Remember that progress is about being a *better* performer or composer, and that both are supported by students becoming *more sophisticated* listeners.

Ofsted curriculum pillars

Ofsted's *Music Subject Report* (Sept 2023) also talks about three core 'pillars of progression':

Technical	Constructive	Expressive
• How to control sound • How to read notation	• Musical elements • Components of composition	• Quality • Musical meaning • Creative output
Make Music	Think About Music	Become a Musician

You can look at each of these across the disciplines of performing, composing and listening, referencing the 'of', 'how to' and 'about' labels, and the three different kinds of knowledge that have been explored earlier in this chapter.

Performing

The **technical pillar** looks at **how to** make music through:

- gradual, iterative development of motor skills, playing and singing with increasing accuracy and confidence
- **substantive knowledge**, for example being able to read complex rhythms in a range of different clefs
- **disciplinary knowledge**, for example being able to play with a high level of technical agility or being able to use sophisticated compression techniques on a DAW.

The **constructive pillar** looks at **knowledge about** music, through:

- increasingly fluent use of musical elements in performance
- **substantive knowledge**, for example being able to understand and interpret directions to play *tenuto* or with pitch bends
- **disciplinary knowledge**, which could involve being able to play cross-rhythms or subtle variations in articulation.

The **expressive pillar** looks at **knowledge of** music through:

- critical selection of the appropriate techniques to demonstrate understanding of the composer's intentions
- **substantive knowledge**, for example knowing that a piece of music is from the early Baroque period or is a modern reworking of a 1980s Synthpop track
- **disciplinary knowledge**, which could involve being able to switch between *clean* and *overdriven* guitar, being able to accurately interpret a *mordent,* or using a pedal appropriately.

Developing performing skills needs to be built into every scheme of work across every Key Stage so that students can make the appropriate progress in mastering the skills needed to express themselves musically. This will also help progression into your co-curricular programme and on to your courses at Key Stages 4 and 5.

Top tip

There are many schools that like to plan a keyboard skills unit at the start of Year 7. There is obvious value in making sure that all students have a working knowledge of the notes on a keyboard, but not every student in your school is going to identify as a keyboard player. Equally, those students who already play the keyboard may already have the keyboard skills you want them to have. This will be true for any musical instrument you can think of. Rather than setting outcomes that only measure their ability to become increasingly proficient on the instrument, set outcomes that increasingly challenge students' ability to explicitly demonstrate their understanding of musical concepts as a whole.

Composing

If you think about your students as creators or producers of music, it becomes a lot easier to think about composing. Students might sit by themselves and use a whole host of samples or loops and organise them in a particular way to create their own composition. They may also collaborate with others as part of an ensemble, as a pair of vocalists, or as a solo artist with a producer. They might sit with their instrument and create a piece of music, working completely independently. These are all authentic processes, and your curriculum planning will need to help students identify which process is the most appropriate at any one time.

The **technical pillar** in composition is about setting students up with the basic motor skills (and inner ear) to be able to explore and produce ideas. The **knowledge** could involve knowing how to plug your guitar into an audio interface and record a set of chords at the right level over a click track. It could also be about a singer having enough skill to play some chords so they can lay down a framework over which they can sing.

The **constructive pillar** involves:

- knowing and handling the components of composition
- **substantive knowledge**, including the conventions around how music is put together. This can be really effectively taught by working with students to reverse engineer what they are creating or performing so they can understand how everything works. A group ensemble performance activity can be used to experiment with different textures, to consider how melodies and basslines are built from chords, and to show how dynamics can be affected by different instrument combinations, as well as investigating how you play each one
- **disciplinary knowledge**, focussed on developing students' ability to communicate their understanding, either by playing music themselves or directing other people to perform their ideas.

The **expressive pillar** involves:

- increasingly sophisticated and creative musical outcomes
- **substantive knowledge**, which will relate to students' understanding of the conventions associated with particular styles of music
- **disciplinary knowledge**, which is similar to that of the constructive pillar, but which is reliant on students having a more sophisticated technical and substantive understanding about what they are doing.

Top tip

A scheme of work on the blues is a really good way of developing knowledge about the conventions of music, including four-bar phrases, twelve-bar structure, primary chords with a cadence point, the minor pentatonic scale, musical texture, and call-and-response. It also offers lots of opportunities to develop ensemble performance skills, while providing additional opportunities for students to demonstrate increasingly advanced technical skills as they perform within the framework. As you look to put this into your curriculum plan, consider how you can design the scheme so that they are thinking about the **constructive** elements of the music while they work to perform as an ensemble. Then, consider how this same knowledge can be transferred across into your next scheme.

Listening, understanding and appraising

In this context, students are both 'active consumers' and 'passive participants' of music. They will hear lots of music but may actively listen to a lot less. When they are listening, they are likely to be listening to a relatively narrow aspect and will make fairly quick judgements as to whether they wish to engage with the music or not. They may also be a huge fan of a particular artist and may either have a detailed knowledge about how each song has been put together, or very little knowledge of this at all. Any one of us can have a huge appreciation of music without necessarily being able to perform it.

Planning your curriculum to develop listening skills is best approached by looking at the **expressive pillar** first.

The **expressive pillar** is about having an increasing **knowledge of**:

- musical pieces, genres, cultures and quality
- **substantive** facts about music. These can include the musical instruments associated with different genres of music across different cultures, the decade in which a particular style of music emerged, and the name of the chords used in the verse of a song. This fact learning can be set as homework tasks or 'focus' tasks during one portion of a lesson

Chapter 3: Designing your curriculum – musical skills and knowledge

- developing **disciplinary knowledge** requires an additional, more integrated approach. Students need to learn how to apply technical language (music vocabulary) to describe or explain what they hear, as well as learning how to evaluate its quality, how to analyse the way it has been constructed, and how to apply it to their own work to create something of their own.

The **constructive pillar** is about having an increasing **knowledge about** musical elements and their use, including:

- **substantive knowledge**, which is best developed through identifying key things students need to be explicitly thinking about during practical music 'creation' tasks
- **disciplinary knowledge**, which is developed by identifying ways in which you expect students to use technical language about the musical elements in verbal and written responses.

The **technical pillar** is about developing students' knowledge about **how to** listen to pieces of music, including:

- **substantive knowledge**, which will be built around remembering key facts about music
- **disciplinary knowledge**, which will be focussed on how to evolve from hearing a general wash of musical sound to listening out for specific details. This might include listening out for a particular instrument, or recognising the start of a new section based on how the texture or chord pattern changes.

Top tip

Use Bloom's Taxonomy when thinking about how you want your students to become increasingly expressive and sophisticated in the way they talk and write about music. Think also about when you want to use a listening exercise as a stimulus to help them remember a key concept, consolidate their understanding, or learn a new concept. In some situations it may be better to do this using a visual aid or as a practical task.

Notation and visual aids

Music is an aural-first artform but some approaches to music teaching have led to notation-first pedagogies.

Your classroom may consist of students who learn:

- completely by ear or verbal and non-verbal cues
- from staff notation
- from tablature
- from drum notation
- from drum maps or DAW graphic scores
- from piano rolls
- from imitation and memorisation.

These are all authentic ways of learning and so your curriculum plan needs to:

1. recognise the **tacit knowledge** they will bring to your classroom
2. build their **disciplinary knowledge** of other forms of learning
3. identify the **substantive knowledge** that needs to be developed.

Designing a curriculum that exposes students to different forms of notation and approaches to learning will be far more valuable to them and achieve better outcomes than trying to develop a curriculum built around increasingly fluent reading of staff notation.

Visual aids

Here are three different ways of presenting the primary chords of I, IV and V:

Example 1:

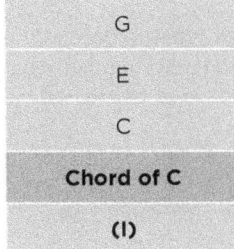 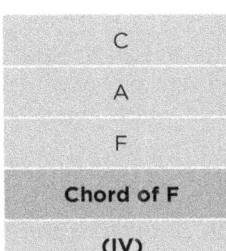 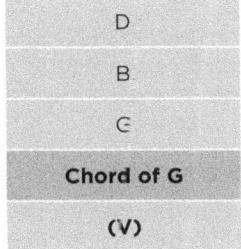

This first example does not rely on any prior knowledge of notation, so can be used to introduce the concept of how triads are constructed and how each chord is related to the others. Removing any other musical notation means you can focus on the key **substantive knowledge** you want students to learn.

Example 2:

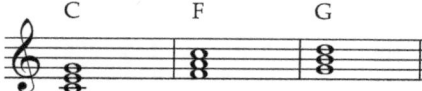

This example builds on the first as a vehicle to support **substantive knowledge** of staff notation, which is useful for all students as you help them to develop a 'working' knowledge of this form of notation.

Example 3:

This final example provides an industry-standard form of notation and starts to connect the theory behind chords to melodic notation without lots of extraneous information, which students will have to be trained 'not to see'.

Notation

When working with notation, consider its purpose, which should be to help students communicate the music they are capable of making as authentically as possible.

A student's ability to perform music may be more advanced than their ability to read staff notation. A chord chart or lead sheet may, therefore, be highly appropriate for a group of students who are learning by ear but need a visual guide to develop their understanding of cadence points or song structure. A simplified arrangement of a piece of music can be useful when introducing aspects of notation but can be counter-productive if the student can already create the same music at a more advanced level. For example, a singer, pianist or drummer might be able to perform using techniques, rhythms and phrases, or in a particular key, that are more aligned to the aural stimulus they've learnt from, but which bear little resemblance to the arrangement they have in front of them. In these cases, there is a risk that they will disengage from the learning process, as the notation they are being asked to play from is preventing them from producing what they see as an authentic version of the music. Equally, asking students to interpret or produce a fully-notated transcription of a crossover dance track is likely to be less useful than supporting them in learning how to read, manipulate and mark-up the same project on a DAW.

The table below provides a summary of Ofsted's curriculum pillars. It may be useful to consider how students' use of different forms of notation can support them in making progress in each of these areas.

	Technical	Constructive	Expressive
Performing	Gradual, iterative development of motor skills; playing and singing with increasing accuracy and confidence.	Increasingly fluent use of musical elements in performance.	Increasing expression in performance and understanding of musical context and provenance.
Composing	Development of motor skills (and the inner ear) to enable exploration and production of ideas.	Knowledge and handling of the components of composition.	Increasing sophistication and creativity in musical outcomes.
Listening	Development of the inner ear.	Conscious awareness of musical elements and their use.	Increasing knowledge of musical pieces, genres, cultures and quality.

Chapter 3: Designing your curriculum – musical skills and knowledge

Chapter 4

Designing your curriculum – assessment and tracking

In this chapter you will learn how to approach assessment and tracking to make sure it is meaningful to you and your stakeholders.

The purpose of assessment

As subject leader, you will need to consider how you are assessing students and why:

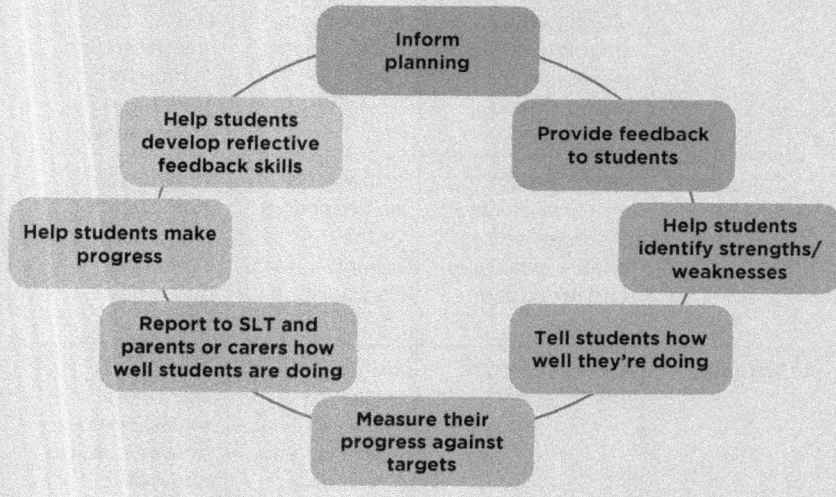

Curriculum and assessment in music education – the research context (Fautley and Daubney, 2019) identifies four aspects to do with the purpose of assessment:

1. To sit alongside learning and provide advice
2. To provide a judgement on the extent of a student's learning
3. To measure how much a student has achieved
4. To measure how good what they have achieved is

Your curriculum planning and assessment needs to identify the quantity you expect students to cover, the quality of their outcomes and whether these things are behind, ahead or at the level you would expect at any given moment.

Types of assessment

Asking yourself what type of assessment to use may seem like an obvious question, but it will be useful to think about as you work out how to make your assessment practices fit within your whole-school policies and assessment calendars. When the National Curriculum was first introduced in 1988, the task group on assessment and teaching categorised four **types** of assessment:

Formative: Positive achievements of students are recognised and discussed and the appropriate next steps may be planned.

Diagnostic: Learning difficulties may be scrutinised and classified so that appropriate help and guidance can be provided.

Summative: Recording of the overall achievement of the students in a systematic way.

Evaluative: Some aspects of the work of a school, an LEA or other discrete part of the education service can be assessed and/or reported upon.

The formative and diagnostic terms may be more commonly recognised as 'Assessment for Learning' but your school may use different terminology to mean the same thing.

Across each of these four areas, you will be looking at the development of students' substantive knowledge alongside their disciplinary knowledge. At any given moment in a lesson, your student will either be demonstrating the acquisition of a new piece of knowledge or an improvement in how they are using an existing piece of knowledge. Being able to distinguish between these two different things when providing formative and diagnostic feedback will be key to getting an accurate picture of how each student is getting on.

Chapter 4: Designing your curriculum – assessment and tracking

Who is it for?

Students: within the classroom, your assessment is primarily formative and diagnostic so that your students can understand what they already know and how they can develop further.

Parents or carers: like your students, they are interested in how their child is getting on, how this compares to where they should be and what is in place to keep them moving forward. This information is likely to be a summative assessment of the formative and diagnostic assessments you have been making.

SLT: SLT will use the assessment data you have gathered to make an **evaluative** decision on how well students within music are achieving against pre-defined targets. It is most likely that this will be a comparison involving the **summative** data you have provided for a particular year group following some form of 'assessment window' or 'data drop'.

Ofsted, exam boards, governors, LEA, academy executive: these will use data from the school to make evaluative decisions about how well student cohorts are achieving compared to pre-defined targets and to identify any particular positive or negative trends.

As subject leader, you will need to plan your curriculum so that you can gather a range of formative and diagnostic information which, when pulled together, provides an accurate summative report of how your students are developing. This will then provide you with a robust system that can be explained to others as needed.

Managing your assessment data and tracking progress

It can sometimes feel as if the need to generate evaluative whole-school data at particular moments dictates how you plan your curriculum. If you design your curriculum to generate lots of 'moments' to track students' development of substantive and disciplinary knowledge, then you can create a process that looks a little like this:

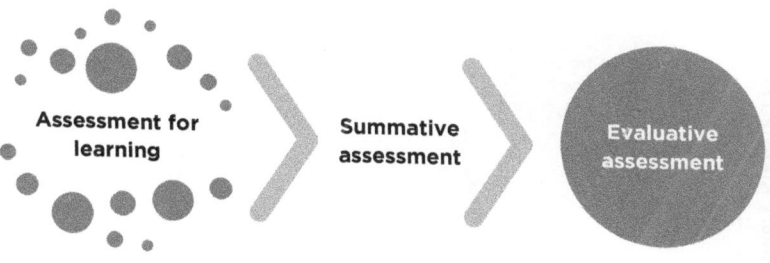

The next step is to consider the linear progression pathway you are creating for your students and how their progress sits on top of this.

There will be a number of times in your curriculum plan where you will need to challenge students to acquire new skills.

You may start with an activity where a drummer demonstrates their performing knowledge. You may follow this with an activity where they have to demonstrate their ability to construct a chord sequence on the keyboard. These are both relevant to the songwriting process, but if you were to compare the 'grades' they got for each activity, it could look as if they have gone backwards. At the same time, you may challenge a Grade 3 pianist to focus on improvising an accompaniment from a lead sheet in the first activity and then move them on to the same chord construction exercise in the second. In this situation, you may find that their first 'grade' is lower than people would expect from a 'Grade 3 student' but their second 'grade' shows that they have moved forwards.

The activities may be carefully sequenced within your curriculum to develop the skills they need but the summative snapshot may tell a confusing story, like this:

Measuring progress

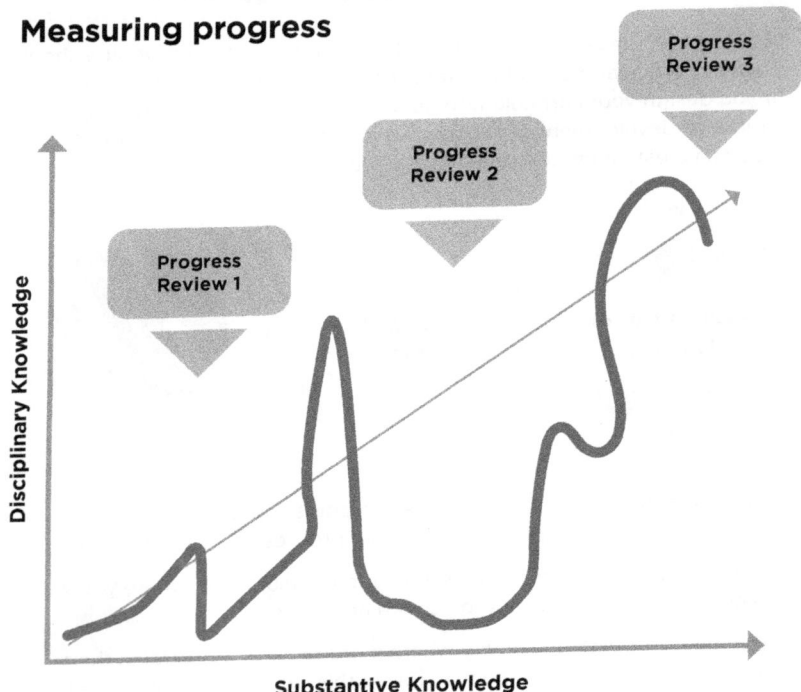

As you design your curriculum, identify where students will demonstrate the following:

1. the academic acquisition of a piece of knowledge
2. the practical acquisition of a new skill
3. the appropriate application of that knowledge of the skill to the task.

You can then create a series of moments where you and your students can track their acquisition of substantive, disciplinary and threshold concepts, which gradually, iteratively and coherently accumulate across the three curriculum pillars.

Formative and diagnostic assessment

This type of assessment is designed to provide evaluations of ongoing work and to set numerous short-term targets.

It can take many forms:
- verbal feedback
- a reflective discussion
- advice and guidance given by someone else on developing specific techniques
- a brief piece of written guidance on how to move forward
- observations of students at work and the technical language they are using to communicate
- pieces of homework
- responses to questions.

This assessment sits at classroom level and, as the subject expert, you have the authority to design what it looks like so it can provide meaningful information for you, your team and your students.

You may decide to use digital or physical books where students can write down their next steps based on the feedback they receive. You might generate booklets where there is space to do the same. The 'notes' section in many DAWs can also be a good place for students to record this data.

Top tip

Shared progress trackers, used consistently across your sequenced lessons, are a useful way of building up the picture you need. The following pages provide an example of this linked to the 'Building your band' scheme from Chapter 3. It uses simple tickboxes so that students can identify when they have demonstrated a particular piece of knowledge and where they have consolidated this knowledge through a later task.

Chapter 4: Designing your curriculum – assessment and tracking

Progress tracker

Instrument skills	Yes	Confidently	Score
Can play notes on the bass guitar using tab			
Can play notes on the guitar using tab			
Can play chords on the guitar using a chord chart			
Can play chords on the piano using a chord chart			
Ensemble skills			
Can play notes in time with others/to a click track			
Can play rhythms in time with others/to a click track			
Can sing or play melodies in time with others/to a click track			
Can use dynamics to balance my part with everyone else			
Can explain what role my instrument plays in the group (melody, accompaniment/chords, bass, rhythm, and so on)			
Style skills			
Can change the rhythm to create a different style			
Can change the articulation to create a different sound			
Can change how I play chords to create a different sound			
Song knowledge skills			
Can work out how to play a chord sequence from a chord chart			
Can work out a chord sequence using I, ii, iii, IV, V, and vi			

Instrument skills	Yes	Confidently	Score
Can explain how many bars long the introduction, verse, chorus and bridge are			
Can explain a 12-bar blues structure			
Can explain a 32-bar song form structure			
Songwriting skills			
Can record a bassline in time to a click track			
Can record a chord sequence in time to a click track			
Can record a melody in time to a click track			
Can use different chord sequences to create an intro, verse and chorus			
Can select notes of the chord to create melodies			
Can select notes of the chord to create basslines			
Advanced skills			
Can work out how to play more complex chords using accidentals and/or 7ths			
Can work out how to play songs in a different key			
Can create contrast in songs by changing the tonality (key)			
Can create development in the texture of songs by adding or removing instrumental layers			

The score then provides a total number, which can be plugged into a department tracker so you can measure each student against appropriate whole-school data and report to the wider community.

Summative assessment

This type of assessment takes place when achievement has to be reported and is used to measure progress against pre-defined parameters. At Key Stage 3, the assessment criteria are designed by you but the target they are working towards will not be.

The data you provide that reports the summative assessment is likely to be made much more reliable by collating cumulative data over time, as opposed to through a single, final assessment. These assessment principles remain true for courses at Key Stages 4 and 5, where students have to produce final performance and composition coursework for assessment. As a teacher, you are able to mark their work far more accurately if you have maintained an awareness of the processes they have gone through. You will also be able to monitor and report on their progress with greater accuracy if you focus on the specific types of knowledge they are developing at any given moment.

Top tip

Take a look at the published criteria for the courses you are running at Key Stages 4 and 5 and break down their criteria into substantive and disciplinary knowledge. This will help you to sequence a holistic and coherent curriculum plan and assessment tracker even where you may be sharing different aspects of the course with other teachers. It is also a really helpful way of developing other stakeholders' understanding of what knowledge the students they are working with need to develop.

Building an accurate picture

Your curriculum planning will be designed to develop new knowledge and consolidate pre-existing knowledge. Your assessments will give you an ongoing and developing picture of the progress your students are making. Your recording of this information and data will enable you to communicate this picture effectively and build an archive of media which you can refer back to and share. This media archive is likely to be built up of audio and video recordings, logbooks, knowledge tests and reflective feedback notes.

Underpinning all of these will be a tracking grid, which you can use to create a cumulative linear measure of progress even if the learning experiences themselves are not linear.

Putting students at the centre

As subject leader you will need to design your assessment processes to adhere to your school's assessment policy. Whatever approach you take, remember to put the student at the centre, as their own ability to identify how well they are developing as musicians will be the most effective vehicle to developing music at your school. The checks you can make are:

- Students can talk about music.
- Students can reflect on their work.
- Students can differentiate between their substantive and disciplinary knowledge.
- Students can refine their work.
- Students can adapt their work.
- Students can define their progress in relation to the above.

Chapter 5

Supporting your colleagues with music

In this chapter you will learn how to take a supportive approach to developing your colleagues' confidence and skill in teaching music, whatever their level of musical skill.

Supporting the specialists within your department

Even if all the members of your department are music specialists, they will not all be specialist in every form of music! If you are going to deliver the curriculum and co-curricular programme effectively then you will need to ascertain your colleagues' skill sets by carrying out a skills audit.

This could take a number of forms to suit your own school, but the most logical way to approach this might be to ask each teacher to complete a self-assessment survey based on the contents of the music national curriculum, your own curriculum plan, and your co-curricular programme. You'll also want to give them some free space to tell you about any areas of expertise they have that are not currently reflected in your school's music offer, which will give you ideas for future development.

Identifying staff skill priorities

Once all your colleagues have completed their self-assessment skills audit you will want to turn all this data into a set of priorities, which can form the basis of an action plan. If you are lucky, your colleagues will all have identified the same areas for development, which will make the job a lot easier!

If the responses are more mixed, you will need to make some tough decisions about who and what to prioritise. To do this, you will want to think of the following factors:

- **Quick wins:** what can you fix almost instantly to make an impact on teaching quality?
- **Vision:** which issues will impact most negatively on the delivery of your vision?
- **School improvement:** which issues align most closely to the aims of your SIP (school improvement plan)?
- **Fundamentals:** which basic issues need to be fixed first?
- **Staffing teams:** who will benefit most, and who will they then be able to support in turn?

This will help you to sort the areas for development into priority order, and then you can start at the top of the list this year and work your way down. You will want to come up with a range of development strategies that will address your priority areas succinctly and efficiently without overloading your colleagues. It is important too that you discuss your proposals with the teachers involved to find out whether they agree that your idea is the best way of providing them with support. If your colleagues feel they are being made to do something that isn't going to have the impact that they want, they are less likely to buy into the whole process, which may mean that you go to a lot of effort for very little return.

This process will feed into your music development plan, on which you can find more information in Chapter 8.

Top tip

The key thing to remember, as always, is that you are only one person, and there is only so much you can do in one year! As long as you have identified all the 'problems' that need fixing and are working towards solving some of them, then you are on top of your responsibilities as a subject leader.

Reading recommendation

Published in 2016, the DfE's *Standard for Teachers' Professional Development* guidance is a useful starting point for ensuring that the development opportunities that you provide for your colleagues will be impactful.

Monitoring and developing colleagues' teaching

In order to carry out successful observations on your colleagues, you should approach this process imagining it was yourself being observed. How would you want it to work? What would you want to get out of it? What would put you at ease?

Establish a supportive and non-judgemental tone from the outset, making it clear that the purpose of the observation is to support professional growth, celebrate effective practice, and improve outcomes for students across your department. Share the criteria or focus areas in advance so that the teacher knows what to expect, and ensure these align with the department's goals or school-wide priorities. This transparency helps reduce anxiety and builds trust, creating a foundation for constructive feedback and collaboration.

During the observation, take a holistic view of the lesson, considering both its structure and the students' engagement and learning. Pay attention to how the teacher adapts their approach to meet diverse student needs, the clarity of their instructions, and the level of challenge provided. Rather than focusing solely on what could be improved, actively note examples of effective strategies or creative methods they employ. Be objective and open-minded, understanding that different teaching styles can achieve excellent results. Record specific evidence to support your feedback, such as key moments when students demonstrated understanding or responded enthusiastically to the lesson.

After the observation, prioritise a reflective and collaborative feedback discussion. Start by inviting the teacher to share their thoughts on how the lesson went, fostering self-evaluation and ownership of their practice. Share positive observations first, highlighting strengths and successful techniques, before gently addressing areas for improvement with actionable suggestions.

Use language that emphasises development, such as, 'One idea to consider might be...' or, 'It could be helpful to try...'. End the conversation with an opportunity for the teacher to ask questions or share insights, and agree on next steps or goals to reinforce the observation's value as a constructive and forward-looking process.

> ### Top tip
>
> Everyone is probably familiar with the idea that you should sandwich a piece of negative feedback between two pieces of positive feedback. However, research suggests that you actually need a much higher ratio of positive to negative feedback in order to improve performance. Try to aim for around five or six positive feedback points for every negative point, so that the teacher leaves motivated to build on the great work they're already doing, rather than feeling like they shouldn't bother because they are terrible at their job!

Supporting instrumental specialists

Depending on how your instrumental teachers are employed, you may or may not be officially responsible for their professional development and the quality of their teaching. If this is your responsibility then you should involve them in the skills audit. You will probably want to know how equipped they feel to support students studying for GCSE, A Level or Vocational Qualifications, and it would definitely be useful to know if they have any undisclosed talents that could feed into your co-curricular plans for the future.

Even if you are not directly responsible for the instrumental team in this way, you will still want to support them day to day. You can find out more about ways to do this in Chapter 6.

Supporting non-specialists

At the time of writing, in the UK at least, there is a significant shortage of specialist music teachers. This means that many schools rely on some or all of their music being taught by non-specialist staff, or in music being taken off the timetable entirely until a suitable teacher can be employed. But the very fact that you're reading this book suggests that this is probably not the case in your school.

If you do have non-specialists teaching music in your school, or if you are one yourself, the first thing to say is 'don't panic!' Despite what you might have been led to believe, it is actually perfectly possible for non-specialists to deliver decent music teaching at Key Stage 3. All they need is a confidence boost and the right support and professional development in place.

Developing non-specialists' musical confidence

It might be a slight exaggeration to say that the biggest problem non-specialist teachers face is lack of confidence, but that opinion is not far off the mark. It is not just a lack of subject-specific teacher training that causes a lack of confidence in non-specialist teachers; the problem goes deeper than that, right back to their own school days. Most people across the Western world adopt a philosophy of 'talent' being the key to 'musicianship'. By giving some children additional lessons on instruments; by holding auditions for choirs and ensembles; by handing out certificates in assemblies and selecting certain children to perform as soloists,

Top tip

When dealing with teacher confidence as a subject leader, it may be useful to think about what you would say to a student in the same position. You would never want students to think that they weren't 'talented' or 'good enough' to take part in music, and you would make every effort to encourage and support them. You know that the majority of students are able to achieve against every aspect of the music curriculum, and therefore it logically follows that their teachers, with all those extra years of experience and learning, are capable of that, too.

you can unintentionally give the impression that music is only for 'special' or 'talented' children, and that everyone else is 'unmusical'. These kinds of special, elective activities traditionally require the learning of notation, which places another barrier between the 'musical' and 'unmusical' children. Teachers who have grown up through this system will often therefore identify themselves as 'unmusical' purely on the basis that they do not play an instrument or read music.

This complex, multi-layered confidence problem cannot be instantly fixed. You can't go on a course or take part in a music staff meeting and magically decide you are 'musical', after all. As a music subject leader it is important to listen to staff articulate *if* and *why* they don't feel confident. Often you will find that with some probing you can uncover some misconceptions about what music teaching actually involves, or specific areas of the curriculum that feel like a step too far for some of your teachers.

Top tip

If you are dealing with low levels of confidence among your colleagues, start with listening to music. This requires no specialist musical 'talent' and in fact, if the listener doesn't 'get' what the composer or artist was intending, it could be argued that it is the composer's/artist's fault, not the listener's! Ask your colleagues to share their favourite piece of music and say why they like it. This conversation should help you to draw out the fact that music is for everyone, and that all opinions are valid.

Developing non-specialists' musical skills

If a lack of confidence is preventing your colleagues from teaching music, then creating an all-singing, all-dancing scheme of work designed for non-specialist teachers could be just the ticket. Having a fully-resourced scheme to work from means that teachers don't have to worry about designing their lessons and looking for supporting materials, they simply follow the instructions provided.

Top tip

If your school is in England and you are subject to an Ofsted inspection, the inspector may want to establish that teachers know where their lessons are coming from and going to in terms of progression, so you will need to move beyond a model where teachers load up the next lesson plan and teach what is prescribed without thinking about the context of the scheme as a whole.

Schemes of work can really help boost teachers' confidence and show them that they *can* teach music, but in the long term you will want to develop their skills further so that they can start to create their own lessons and supporting materials. This will take the pressure off you as subject lead, since you will be able to scale back on how much planning and resourcing you do for other people.

As part of the skills audit discussed above you will have ascertained the areas that your non-specialist colleagues are most worried about and can put a plan in place to address these over time. Sometimes, however, non-specialists feel like they are not equipped in any way to teach music, so it can be difficult to know where to start with a support plan. In this instance, it would be wise to start with developing the teacher's own basic musical skills, rather than their music teaching skills. Help them to develop their understanding of terminology, show them how to use instruments and music technology resources, and allow them to practise the things that they need to demonstrate in upcoming units with you to support and guide them. Once they have mastered the basics, the next step would ideally be to observe you or other specialist colleagues in action so they can see what good music teaching should look like. Over time, especially if you're able to give them the same unit to teach multiple times, their confidence and skill will grow and they will become a 'specialist' in their little bit of the music curriculum.

Reporting to non-specialist SLT

It is inevitable that most of us will end up with a line manager who is not a music specialist, and this can cause significant issues if they don't understand how music teaching 'works.' Hopefully your Senior Leadership Team (SLT) will trust your professionalism to tell them what is and isn't working, and manage your subject as you see fit, but if you run into any difficulties then there are some strategies that you can use to bridge the understanding gap.

It will help to communicate with SLT on a level that they do understand, so wherever possible try to relate what you are doing in music to wider school priorities, such as those in your school improvement plan. This will help to avoid SLT feeling uncomfortable and defensive. Using phrases like, 'I know we are working towards X in the school improvement plan, and for us in music we're achieving this by doing Y', and then going on to give clear examples and explanation, will help to put your line manager at ease and ensure they understand the approaches that you are taking.

You will need to advocate for your subject whenever possible, outlining the approaches you are taking, the skills and knowledge students are developing, and how you are supporting whole-school policies and agendas. Don't be afraid to step up at the first opportunity if initiatives and ideas are announced that are going to be problematic for music; it's much easier to intervene at the 'design' stage of an idea than when the idea has already been fully formed and signed off by SLT!

Top tip

Nobody likes to feel that their expertise is being called into question. When speaking to SLT, frame your concerns as collaborative problem-solving opportunities rather than critiques. Use phrases like, 'I would really value your support with implementing this idea across the music department', to show respect for their expertise while still giving yourself the opportunity to point out that music needs thinking about differently from other subjects. By presenting your concerns as areas where SLT can make a positive difference, you avoid sounding like you are criticising everything!

Chapter 5: Supporting your colleagues with music

One of the areas that can cause the most difficulty is observations by non-specialist SLT. Most SLT, when pressed about their ability to observe music, will say something along the lines of, 'I don't know about music teaching, but I do know what good teaching looks like'. In a best-case scenario this means you end up with an observation report that has general feedback about things like behaviour management, questioning strategies and so forth. In a worst case you end up with feedback telling you to do things that are impossible, or detrimental to musical learning. If you feel that your observation process would benefit from some specialist input, there are a few strategies you could try:

- When it is time for your observation, ask if a specialist can be invited, maybe a music specialist SLT member from another school that you partner with, a manager from the local music service or music hub, or another member of SLT from your own school who is not your line manager but does have a music specialism. Frame this as an opportunity for you to learn from a specialist, rather than what it actually is: an opportunity for your line manager to be upskilled!
- Invite a member of SLT to sit in on an observation that you are carrying out on one of your departmental colleagues (with that colleague's permission and agreement, of course). For schools in England, you could ask for this on the basis of 'Ofsted training', as it mirrors the process of a 'deep dive' observation with you sitting alongside the inspector. Again this looks like you asking for support that will benefit you, but really it's an opportunity for you to show SLT what sort of things a specialist looks for when observing a lesson.
- Request a peer observation process, asking if another department head from a different school can come and observe you, and vice versa. This will be a useful process for you anyway, and makes you look proactive about your own professional development. It will also give you an observation record to compare to the observations carried out by SLT so that you can point out any discrepancies in the event that you are being 'marked down' for something that your line manager doesn't understand.

In my experience, in any given school half of SLT are PE teachers. There's nothing wrong with PE teachers of course, but if your SLT is unbalanced and doesn't represent the full range of faculties, then this can cause communication and expectation issues right across the school. Don't be afraid to make (respectful) suggestions when SLT positions come up for recruitment: 'Wouldn't it be great to have a performing arts specialist for this position? That would be a really strong addition to the team!'

Chapter 6

Defining your co-curricular programme

In this chapter you will learn how to create a 'co-curricular' programme that is sustainable, supports student development, and is understood and celebrated by the school community.

Defining the purpose of your co-curricular and instrumental programme

Young people spend more time outside your classroom than in it and, by extension, engage with the music they like far more in their own time than with you there. This is an important consideration when working out what your department should provide in the time you have available. It may seem obvious, but the approach should be similar to that of planning your curriculum. Refer back to Chapters 3 and 4 for a reminder.

Unlike your curriculum, your co-curricular programme can be made up of many different things that may or may not happen on a weekly basis. It can consist of:
- formal ensembles organised on a timetable
- informal access to facilities in the school

- instrumental tuition
- workshops organised outside curriculum time for students
- external visits and tours
- performances and presentations.

Top tip

You will want to be able to see the development of skills that help your students to define and express their musical identity both individually and collectively. Your programme as a whole should:

- support both less able and more able students in developing their skills
- provide a means to widen students' understanding of musical genres
- provide a space for students to explore their musical identity
- have an impact on the quality of engagement and academic outcomes in your curriculum.

Audit your offer

As you look at your current offer, ask yourself the following questions to help you shape how you want things to look in the future:

- Who is the activity for?
- What skills are being developed?
- How is this development being measured and shared?
- Who is running the activity?
- Where and when is it being run?

Who is the activity for?

Whether you are running a weekly orchestra, band rehearsal sessions, sound recording workshops, brass tuition, or preparing for a mass performance at an external venue, it is important to keep track of which students are attending and what benefit they are getting from attending. It's even more important to look at whether you are duplicating the same type of offer for the same type of students or providing opportunities that are being accessed by different cohorts.

What skills are being developed?

There is a long list of skills that could be developed, depending on the activity, including: social interaction and leadership skills; listening and ensemble skills; advanced technical skills linked to mastering a particular instrument. It may be that the activity covers a broad range of skills or is designed to focus on one key area. In any case, you should be able to define with the ensemble leader what these skills are and demonstrate exactly how they will be developed through the planned activity. You should also be able to link these skills back to your music development plan and your curriculum, ensuring that they are appropriate for the students attending.

How is this development being measured and shared?

Your audit should identify whether the key measure is a public performance, an increase in active involvement, or an increase in academic outcomes. Not every activity warrants a public performance, but where it does, use this as an opportunity to verify that the students involved have improved their skills rather than simply spending their time preparing for a performance. In other areas, you'd hope to see regular attendance to the activity itself, alongside an increase in their voluntary engagement in other activities, improvements in the quality of their work in the curriculum, and an increase in the number of students opting for your subject at Key Stages 4 and 5.

Who is running the activity?

Whether you are a one-person department or managing a large team, you will be working with colleagues with different levels of capacity, motivations and lived experiences of co-curricular activity. Instrumental teachers who are highly skilled at preparing individual students for instrumental exams may be very skilled at running ensembles where the focus is on preparing set repertoire with a high level of detail.

> ### Example
>
> **Beginner guitar club; Tuesday lunchtime**
>
> Designed for any student who has never had formal lessons on the guitar. You'll be introduced to reading chord charts and tab alongside lead and rhythm-playing techniques so you can perform songs as part of a group. Ongoing attendance will also help you understand how songs are put together so you can write your own.

Chapter 6: Defining your co-curricular programme

By contrast, there will be others who are highly skilled at working with mixed ability groups who learn by ear through organic collaboration. This will affect the direction of the activities and the impact they will have on different students.

Where and when is it being run?

There will be a number of factors influencing when certain activities take place. A regular workshop for GCSE students might helpfully take place in the spring term of Year 10 as this aligns best with the current curriculum map. An external visit to a live event for Year 9 might helpfully take place in the autumn term as it is part of the process of selling the subject ahead of students picking their subject options. Keyboard Club might run on a Monday lunchtime as this fits in with the visiting music teacher's timetable. You may need to consider the space being used and decide whether it is more beneficial to have the practice rooms set aside for individual music tuition or used for small group rehearsals at different points in the day. Your school day will also impact when activities can take place and how many you can run. If your school runs a split lunch, then activities that cater for students across multiple year groups may be better run after school hours while you reserve lunchtimes for focussed activities with specific cohorts. Whether you are inheriting a co-curricular programme, or building one from scratch, it is worth remembering the BRAN principle when looking to make changes:

Benefit	What positive impact will changing the activity have?
Risk	What risks will be posed to attendance, staffing, and quality by changing it?
Alternative	How else could the activity be run? Where else could it be run? What could be run in its place?
Nothing	What will happen if you do nothing?

Top tip

As the leader of music in your school, your core priority is the delivery of high-quality outcomes. You are required to do this across a set number of hours, while also having to set aside for non-contact time for your teachers. You may find that you will be able to achieve better outcomes by negotiating set time on your timetable to run activities, such as small group tuition for target cohorts, rather than trying to squeeze things into a short lunch break.

Instrumental tuition

This could be a whole chapter in itself, but, in essence, many of the same principles apply to instrumental tuition as to the rest of your departmental programme.

The key difference is that individual instrumental tuition has its own curriculum and exam ecosystem. Typically, individual students receive one-to-one coaching from a highly trained professional in order to become increasingly specialised in one musical discipline, performing as a soloist on a musical instrument from within the Western classical or pop traditions. Unsurprisingly, this level of coaching comes at a price and, if you're in the UK, it's worth keeping an eye on the annual survey of instrumental teaching rates conducted by the Independent Society of Musicians (www.ism.org) to see what these charges are across the UK.

As subject leader, you are likely to find yourself in one of three positions:

1. Self-employed teachers

Individual teachers invoice the parents or carers of students directly to deliver one-to-one coaching to individual students. They use your building as the venue for this tuition. The school has no involvement in this contractual relationship.

2. Third-party arrangement

An external company, such as a music hub or other provider, enters into an agreement to provide teachers to deliver an agreed number of hours of tuition across an agreed range of instruments or activities. The external company will have their own agreement with the individual teachers setting out their terms and status of employment.

Chapter 6: Defining your co-curricular programme

3. Directly employed teachers

The school directly employs the instrumental teachers.

There are advantages and disadvantages to each set-up and some of these are captured in the table below:

Employment Status	Advantages	Disadvantages
Self-employed instrumental teacher	• School only required to fulfil obligations around keeping children safe in education and workers' rights • All administration managed by the instrumental teacher	• No control over directed time • No control over rates of pay • No control over quality assurance • No direct control over lesson content
Third-party arrangement	• Outside agency responsible for safeguarding and all matters relating to employment • Service level agreement can agree quality assurance and type of delivery • Flexibility to invoice school or individual students	• Limited control over rates of pay • Limited control over directed time • Limited control over availability
Directly employed teacher	• Control over directed time • Control over quality assurance and curriculum delivery • Control over rates of pay	• All on-costs associated with employment are borne by the school • Wholly responsible for all admin and quality assurance

As Secondary music leader, you will need to decide which is best for your school and liaise closely with your HR and Finance Teams to make sure the appropriate model can be put in place.

Visiting teachers are an invaluable resource and you will need to decide how much you want to direct this provision towards one-to-one coaching, small group tuition or ensemble delivery. Working with an outside provider to develop teachers with the right skills to deliver the outcomes you want will be really rewarding, but you need to proceed with caution.

Fees and charges

Unless the teacher is employed directly by the school, the cost of the provision will need to be borne by someone. This can be passed directly on to parents or carers or it may be something that the school can fund through, for example, pupil-premium. In my experience, high-quality small group tuition funded by the school can be an excellent vehicle to achieve a number of whole-school and music development goals. Just remember that as soon as the school gets involved in these financial transactions, it will be reasonable to expect you to monitor the provision closely to ensure value for money.

Employment law

Schools are data-rich places and it can be very tempting to monitor, measure and manage what your visiting teachers are doing. However, it is important to remember that there are strict laws in place to ensure that organisations do not impose unreasonable practices on self-employed professionals – and vice versa. The introduction of IR35 (the UK government's off-payroll working rules) has meant that there are risks associated with 'directing' visiting teachers to complete certain tasks or deliver things at specific times. Any organisation entering into a formal agreement with an individual needs to understand these regulations and so you should ensure that your HR team is able to navigate this for you.

Monitoring, measuring and managing quality and impact

Your students are giving up their time to attend your co-curricular programme and the school is providing the resources for them to be there. You and your team are also using your time to be there. Therefore, you need to be able to guarantee that whatever is planned is providing a worthwhile return on this investment.

As subject leader, you will want to take a holistic view of who is engaging with the co-curricular activity in your school. You will want to measure how many *different* students are making use of the opportunities you have put in place and how many of the *same* students are making more and more use of the opportunities.

From a leadership perspective, you will need to look at the breadth of engagement:

1. What percentage of your school population is engaging?
2. Where the same students are engaging, how diverse is what they're engaging in?

At a managerial level, you will need to look at the quality of what is on offer:

1. How many students are consistently attending?
2. How many new students are joining at the start of each term?
3. How good is the outcome?

Quite often, measuring the quality and impact is simply a 'noticing' exercise, for example picking up on a particular student who is starting to show a particular interest or less interest – sensing a particular vibe or atmosphere.

Top tip

In order to build capacity for informal music activity, try to arrange for the music department to be put on the general staff duty rota – or hand the responsibility over to student leaders – so that the department can remain open without you being solely responsible for monitoring everything. Organise a simple booking system for the rooms using a basic sign-up sheet so you can track who is making use of the space and what they're using it for.

On a formal level, taking registers of attendance at rehearsals and when students make use of the rooms outside lessons is the most effective way of monitoring and tracking the breadth, depth and quality of engagement.

It is relatively rare to be able to formally observe co-curricular provision and set targets, unless this has been agreed as part of a contracted member of staff's performance management. In most situations, monitoring delivery will come down to agreeing the purpose of the activity for an identified cohort and following the steps stated earlier. If you have outsourced the activity to a third party, such as your local music hub, a private organisation or an external workshop company, make sure that you have agreed what their quality assurance measures are and what course of action can be taken should you wish to address the quality of their provision. This should be written into a service level agreement that the school signs with the outsourced provider.

Celebrating your co-curricular programme

The main function of a public performance is to celebrate the learning that has gone on up to that point. Make sure that these are truly representative of your school community and are not always just the 'best' of what is being delivered by a small group of the most 'elite' musicians. These types of concerts are important for many reasons but run the risk of presenting a false impression of what 'normal' music-making looks like. As you're planning your programme of events, consider what you want your key audiences (friends, prospective parents or carers and students, colleagues and/or existing students) to see.

Find opportunities to present the work of students across the age and ability range and make sure these can be presented internally more regularly than they are externally. You can get significant 'buy-in' from other colleagues by providing student-led music for weekly assemblies and year group celebration events, and there is huge value to be gained from putting on a more informal concert to a year group during the school day where the school community get to experience what you do without having to give up their evening. Bear in mind that these do not always need to be live events. Playing a recording of a composition as students walk into assembly can be a really good option.

Older students performing to younger students can create a good sense of aspiration, while students performing to their peers is a good way of building the musical community within that year group.

Informal lunchtime performances can provide a less stressful environment for some students to perform, particularly when you are supporting students in preparing their performance coursework.

If your school uses a house system, a house music competition led by student house captains is another good way of embedding a musical ethos into the fabric of your school.

Finally, make sure you use opportunities to get messages into the tutor programme and staff briefing to promote what you do, and, where external partners are being paid to come and provide a service, do not be shy about sharing this information with colleagues to minimise the risk of students not being allowed out of lessons to attend.

> **"A high-quality music education depends on effective subject and school leadership ... The wider musical life of a school will be underpinned by staff having time outside their curriculum hours to run the clubs, workshops and trips that provide the memorable experiences central to a life-long love of the subject ... Musical activities are often vertical, which can be hard to manage in a school system that mostly works horizontally (for instance, by year group). Schools with a strong musical culture will find creative solutions to enable music to flourish alongside other subjects.**

Ofsted's *Music Research Review*, published in 2021

Top tip

It can be very easy to overload yourself by trying to provide a wide range of opportunities to every type of student. Remember that not all things need to be formally organised and that you can't do everything at once. Think about what you want things to look like in three to five years' time and refer back to the process in Chapter 1.

Chapter 7

Preparing for the role

In this chapter you will learn what sort of things to consider when creating the environment for your students.

Teaching rooms

The priority for any music department is to ensure students have access to the appropriate equipment to develop their skills through the curriculum. To do this, you need to look at how classes are timetabled across your teaching spaces so that your curriculum plan can be delivered consistently. The scenarios below may well be familiar to you now or may be ones you come across as your department grows in the future.

Scenario 1:

8C and 8F might have music scheduled at exactly the same time. They will both be following the same scheme of work so will need access to the same resources.

7D and 9F might have music scheduled at exactly the same time. They will be following different schemes of work but may need access to similar equipment.

Your Year 11 GCSE class might be scheduled at the same time as 7B. The equipment you have available will impact on what content you decide to cover in that lesson each week.

The equipment they need could be:
- keyboards and pianos
- computers running music software
- acoustic, electric and bass guitars
- other stringed instruments
- drum kits, West African drums, tabla, dhol or taiko drums, samba kits, or other untuned percussion
- classroom tuned percussion
- brass instruments
- woodwind instruments
- DJ and performance technology equipment
- microphones
- a mixing desk
- jack, XLR and USB leads
- headphones.

You may be able to buy and store two or more class sets of each, in which case the design and delivery of your curriculum will be quite straightforward. Alternatively, you may need to design your curriculum so that students can develop knowledge through equipment that varies from lesson to lesson. The 'Building your band' example on pages 22 and 23 has been designed so that students can develop their understanding of timing through playing instruments together *or* through recording in time to a click track. They can demonstrate their understanding of structure and texture through playing instruments together *or* through how they organise software instruments in a DAW. This means there is flexibility in what equipment they use without compromising the sequence of learning.

Practice rooms

A music department needs to have dedicated spaces for students to make music together. While your classrooms should be set up to facilitate practical work, you also need to consider noise levels. When you have divided your class into small groups, it's important to give them a dedicated space where they can hear each other. Practice rooms are an essential resource as you are reducing the overall noise level in the main classroom while also providing a space for students with aural hypersensitivity.

Practice rooms are also useful for students to do individual practice as part of their preparation for formal assessment. In the UK, there is no requirement from Ofqual for students to be able to perform as a soloist, but all exam boards at GCSE, IGCSE, IB, A Level and Vocational Level have solo performance units, which students may choose to take (check your syllabus carefully). You may also want to cater for students having one-to-one, paired or small group tuition with a visiting teacher.

What you use your practice rooms for, and when, will impact on what equipment you put in them. It is good practice to dedicate specific equipment to each room, which is reserved for exclusive use in that space.

It is worth noting the guidance around the risk to hearing from exposure to noise. The RNID has some excellent information on its website, rnid.org.uk (search 'How loud is too loud?').

Instruments

Once you've set out your strategic plan for your curriculum and any wider curricular opportunities, you'll be able to decide on what instruments you want your school to own and whether it may be wise to liaise with a local provider, such as your music hub. These organisations are often able to loan instruments to schools for specific projects, particularly when you engage one of their teachers to deliver that project. This could be an 'Endangered Species' programme where teachers deliver lessons to students on instruments with low uptake, such as tuba, double bass or viola. There may be programmes to focus on music from outside the Western classical tradition, such as Carnatic Indian, taiko or Welsh folk music. There could also be Secondary-level Wider Opportunities programmes where students

Chapter 7: Preparing for the role

are given whole-class lessons on violin, clarinet, pBone, and so on. These partnerships are particularly beneficial if you are able to house the instruments in the long term and deliver programmes to different cohorts each year. You may also work with the provider to open up your department outside school hours for a regular ensemble using the loaned equipment for the wider community. In each case, it's vital to ensure that the aims and outcomes of the programme are clear and the teacher delivering has the skills to deliver effectively.

Curriculum instruments: Key Stage 3

Your curriculum is designed to develop your students' ability to access increasingly technical skills and language. As you invest in the equipment, be clear about how it will be used to deepen students' knowledge alongside providing authentic musical experiences.

Keyboards: these are a must-have for any music department. They are an excellent vehicle to help students learn the theory of chords, alongside playing and reading from chord charts and stave notation, and experimenting with a range of timbres. They can also develop a student's ability to accompany themselves and other people. I would recommend investing in MIDI controller keyboards that can be connected to a digital audio workstation (DAW) rather than a set of standalone keyboards.

Guitars: acoustic and electric guitars are also a 'must-have'. Acoustic guitars don't need amps, and a class-set of these will provide your students with cheap and fuss-free access to an instrument on which they can learn how to read and play from chord charts, staff notation and tab. Both keyboards and guitars are equally valuable in helping students to understand scales and modes. Acoustic guitars provide a highly effective way of enabling whole class and small group practical work without generating high levels of noise. I would also recommend investing in a number of electric and bass guitars as these can be connected to a DAW, which will increase the ways in which students can record their creative ideas.

Percussion: a range of percussion is useful for supporting students to understand rhythm, timbre, structure and texture while removing any barriers associated with finding specific pitches on a guitar or keyboard. This percussion may be in the form of a samba kit, dhol or taiko drums, drum pads or any number of other options, depending on what works for your school. Through the visceral hands-on experience of learning how to use these instruments to generate authentic pieces of music, students will be able to develop their understanding of things like:

a) the creative traditions that exist around the relationship between high-pitched sounds and fast rhythms, compared to low-pitched sounds and slow rhythms

b) different textures of music, including homophony, heterophony, polyphony and antiphony

c) structure

d) the impact of instrumentation and playing techniques on dynamics, texture and sonority.

When using percussion alongside notation, remember that an authentic engagement that develops students' disciplinary knowledge of rhythm is likely to involve some complex syncopations and cross-rhythms, which can provide some excellent challenge in decoding a visual stimulus but may limit their own creative output if they are expected to write it down using staff notation.

Orchestral and band instruments: there are some good examples of schools who have invested in class sets of stringed, brass or woodwind instruments to be able to deliver a curriculum that develops students' musical knowledge through playing these melody instruments. This can be highly effective when students are also accessing keyboards, guitars, technology and other instruments to deepen their knowledge. The financial investment may feel significant, but this approach does give students access to an experience that they may not be getting elsewhere and is a good way of generating ensembles through your curriculum. The main consideration is how much of your curriculum you wish to be focussed on these instruments, when providing access to other instruments may be equally valuable. Having a bank of these instruments on long-term loan or in your possession will mean you can target provision for identified students either through the curriculum or a co-curricular project.

Curriculum instruments: Key Stages 4 and 5

Your curriculum for Key Stages 4 and 5 will be shaped by the outcomes set by whichever exam board you are working with. The exam board you choose may well change depending on the needs of each cohort. Every student who has engaged with your curriculum at Key Stage 3 should be equipped with the skills and knowledge to be able to access a GCSE or vocational course. Equally, students who have studied music until the end of Key Stage 4 should have the skills to access a course at Key Stage 5. Each student opting to study at these stages will have their own areas of special interest and this will impact on what exam board and units you select for them to study. The instruments they have had access to before choosing their options will have shaped their areas of interest and you will need to consider how to give them access to increasingly specialist equipment as their skills develop.

Guitars and other portable instruments: where students own or hire their own instruments, it's reasonable to expect them to bring them into school. However, it's useful to invest in some slightly higher-end guitars and amps that can be reserved for more advanced students to use and for use in performances.

The UK government's Assisted Instrument Purchase Scheme allows students at local authority and academy schools to buy instruments net of VAT (search within gov.uk for more information), which can be helpful when students need to invest in higher-quality instruments as they become more advanced.

Pianos, drum kits and other less portable Instruments: you can successfully deliver the curriculum in a department without lots of pianos and drum kits. But clearly some students will want to perform on these instruments, and a high-quality piano will be necessary for accompanying students on other instruments. I would recommend having a 'performance set' that remains 'in situ' in your teaching space and another in your public performance space in order to minimise disruption to your curriculum delivery and minimise risk of damage by moving equipment about. This 'performance set' could comprise:

1. drum kit
2. piano or high-end stage piano
3. bass guitar
4. electric guitar
5. bass, guitar and vocal amps
6. microphones
7. jacks and XLRs.

Depending on the number of practice rooms and their respective sizes, you may wish to set them up so they have the same equipment levels or have them specialise in a particular discipline.

Music technology

For most students, their first engagement with music is via technology. Your curriculum will be enhanced through effective use of technology to support students with both consuming and creating music.

Digital audio workstations (DAWs)

A DAW is any electronic device or software that enables you to record, edit and produce audio files. These are a must-have for your teaching spaces. You will need to choose between using Mac computers or PC computers, and then between desktop or cloud-based software.

Macs are more expensive but have GarageBand installed, which is generally all you need for delivery at Key Stages 3 and 4. You can then invest in Logic Pro X, which is industry-standard music production software and highly recommended for students following any music, sound or digital media production course at Key Stage 5. Macs can be put on a school network, but this can be a slightly more complicated process than with PCs, and can involve investing in further software so some school network managers might be reluctant to do this.

PCs are an equally viable option and may be cheaper. There is no free GarageBand, but PCs are regarded as easier to network and will interact with other Windows software that you may need students to access.

Desktop DAWs are downloaded and installed directly onto your PC or Mac. Ableton Live and FL Studio are considered to be good beginner-friendly options, and some other industry-standard brands are Cubase, Logic Pro X and Pro Tools.

Cloud-based DAWs are paid for via subscription and students access the software online. This means they can collaborate with each other and access their work from any location. The ones you are most likely to have heard of are Soundtrap; BandLab and Soundation.

The option you go for will depend on your budget, personal preference and the needs of your students, but make sure you consider how students are accessing their work. If they have to store their work on the local drive of the machine, they will always have to work on that machine, and you will always have to mark their work there. You can get round this by ensuring that every student has a USB drive on which to save their work, by using a cloud-based solution, or by making sure your computers are on the school network.

You will also need to consider whether you wish to use laptops/ MacBooks or desktops. The obvious advantage of laptops and MacBooks is how portable they are and you can use them to produce music without any additional peripherals (see below), but this does limit the skills and knowledge you can use them to develop.

Peripherals

As mentioned earlier, it is recommended that you set up your teaching space so that you have MIDI controller keyboards attached to a DAW. A MIDI controller keyboard with 49 full-size piano keys (for example the M-Audio Oxygen 49) will look and feel like a traditional keyboard, so it can be used for paired work at Key Stage 3. Students can then log in to the DAW and will have access to the full range of software instruments they need.

You will also need to decide whether you want to use external speakers attached to the computer or headphones. You should equip your department with enough headphone splitters and headphones so that each student can use headphones when working in pairs. At Key Stages 4 and 5, you may prefer students to use their own and use hardwire or Bluetooth to connect.

Ideally, you will also attach an audio interface to each DAW. These are attached to your machine using a USB-C cable and enable students to connect a microphone and/or guitar using the inputs so they can record directly into their DAW.

Recording equipment and studios

A music department that provides students appropriate access to pathways to the music industry will need a basic recording setup. This can range from a DAW on a laptop with a relatively basic audio interface, all the way through to a dedicated recording studio space with a state-of-the-art digital mixing desk. Reputable music equipment suppliers will be able to offer advice on your exact specification based on your budget and space. There are a number of digital mixing desks for under £2,000 that come with a whole range of features and do not take up a lot of space. You should invest in a setup that will look attractive to prospective music production students and can be used effectively by Key Stage 5 students opting for sound production and music technology courses at VQ, IB and A Level.

You will need to resource your department with some basic microphones and stands for everyday use as well as some higher-spec dynamic microphones to be used by individual students to record into

DAWs, and to be used by you and your team to record and present performances. Standard, robust dynamic microphones include:

- Shure SM58: good for vocals
- Shure SM57: good for instruments

For more advanced recording situations, including the content in music technology and sound production courses at Key Stage 5, you'll need to invest in a wider range of microphones so that students can understand how to use specialist microphones for specific scenarios.

A constant and steady supply of XLR leads, jack leads and adaptors will be vital to ensure you can keep everything connected effectively, and you should store your spare supply of these in a secure location while keeping a basic set ready in each classroom and practice room to make set-up for any situation as efficient as possible. Wherever you have a dedicated setup of electric guitar, bass guitar, vocal mic and keyboard, make sure you have a dedicated amp and appropriate lead in the same place.

Storing work and recording progress

As subject leader you will want to decide how you are going to record and store student work. You may want to video the students at work and store the video files centrally to celebrate success and gather evidence of student outcomes. Equipping each teacher with a handheld device or a tablet will be useful for this. You may decide that audio recordings are sufficient, in which case you can use the same DAW setup described earlier to capture their work.

Where students have consistent access to computers, they can also use these to keep notes on their progress, or produce final pieces of work, using digital notebooks, Teams, PowerPoint and Word. Investing in computers that can be used by all students in all lessons could be a very helpful way of reducing the financial and environmental cost of exercise books, printing and photocopying.

Print and digital media

Print media

Printed publications are becoming less common but there is still huge value in using printed materials to support learning. In addition to revision guides for courses at Key Stages 4 and 5, general books about music and the music industry help to generate a 'musical' atmosphere and encourage further reading. Practice music theory papers are really useful as homework or classroom tasks. Musical anthologies or individual pieces of sheet music downloaded from instrumental exam boards or sites like sheetmusicdirect.com are really helpful in a range of contexts.

Digital media

Within your department, students will have ubiquitous access to digital media via your computers. As well as the bespoke music education subscription services, students also have access to a huge online library of music through MuseScore, ultimate-guitar.com, Chordify, IMSLP and elsewhere.

YouTube is filled with video tutorials on how to play particular instruments, how to play particular tracks and how to read music. For aspiring pianists in particular, there is now a way of learning pieces via a live piano roll that is fast becoming a popular way to learn outside of the classroom. As a subject leader, you can embrace the opportunities this presents and also act as a gatekeeper for learning, guiding students to develop all the skills needed to be musicians. This includes making sure they consider the format their music needs to be in to satisfy the requirements of other musicians and exam boards.

The availability of audio and backing tracks online is really helpful, particularly when they are accompanied by a full score.

If your school policy restricts the use of YouTube or the internet, it is strongly recommended that you prepare a clear policy for how you will use these tools safely to discuss with your Senior Leadership Team.

Top tip

The videos on YouTube that show scrolling scores with classical music can be really helpful in softly developing students' score reading skills.

Copyright and licensing

As a subject leader for music, you are working within the music industry and preparing students for work within it. You have a responsibility to support students and colleagues in adhering to the appropriate regulations. However, you cannot expect to be an expert in this complex area and this handbook doesn't claim to make you into one. Within your school, there will be colleagues within the finance and administration teams who will be able to support you in finding the right information and making sure the school can stay within the law.

In most schools in the UK, licensing arrangements have been put in place to ensure that you can:

- play music and videos in lessons including assemblies
- use, photocopy and share certain sheet music within your school for use by students and teachers for educational purposes
- perform copyrighted music.

These are covered under centralised agreements for schools in the UK; more details can be found at copyrightandschools.org.

As a subject leader, you need to ensure that colleagues and students are clear that:

- posting music that is in copyright online without seeking appropriate permission is not allowed
- sharing photocopies of printed music which is in copyright with anyone outside your organisation is not allowed
- schools are given permission to perform musical theatre shows under a specific licence. School versions of musical theatre shows operate under different terms to the full version of shows and deviating from the terms of the licence is not allowed.

Finances and resource management

You may be in a school where a large budget is set aside for use within music. You may be in a school where this is definitely not the case! This will obviously have an impact on how you can resource your department. The guidance stated earlier is designed to suggest a minimum benchmark to ensure you can deliver a broad and balanced curriculum and you should research and set out the cost of investing in and maintaining the resources. Draw on colleagues to support with this and bear in mind that there are also costs attached to maintaining a supply of guitar or violin strings, of plectrums, drum sticks, valve oil, rosin, jack leads, headphone adaptors, music stands and so on.

Where you store equipment will not only impact the efficiency of your lessons but also how long equipment lasts. For each teaching space, including practice rooms, make sure your expectations are clear and followed consistently across your team in three key areas:

1. How will students enter the classroom and access any equipment?
2. How will students end each lesson and pack away any equipment?
3. How will students manage the transition between activities and accessing any equipment?

Make sure these are considered within your curriculum planning and are also clearly managed outside lessons for both formal and informal co-curricular activities.

It is strongly recommended that you set your spaces up to minimise the moving of equipment and to give every resource a dedicated space, so that you and your team can easily monitor its use, location and condition.

This means that each teaching space should have the following:

- a teacher desk with computer running a DAW, audio interface, headphones, MIDI controller, audio playback and microphone
- a drum kit; electric guitar, amp and lead; bass guitar, amp and lead; piano/keys; and vocal mic with amp
- a suite of networked computers, each running a DAW, audio interface, MIDI controller keyboard, audio playback, and two pairs of headphones and splitter

- a suite of acoustic guitars on stands
- a range of untuned percussion.

Practice rooms should have:

- a drum kit; electric guitar, amp and lead; bass guitar, amp and lead; piano/keys; and a vocal mic and amp
- a specialist piano.

Recording studios should have:

- a mixing desk
- microphones
- jack leads and XLRs
- a talkback facility and patch bay
- a sound booth.

And you will need dedicated storage for:

- specialist musical equipment and instruments
- spare materials.

Top tip

Remember that you need to resource the department to deliver the curriculum and provide additional opportunities outside the curriculum. Set out your development plan with a clear view on what is financially viable with the funding you have, what funding you will need from elsewhere, and how you will measure the return on this investment. Remember that very few things can be done for free but that you are working with a team of colleagues who need to provide opportunities that will benefit the students in your care. If the outcomes are clear, there will be people you can work with to find the solution.

Chapter 8

Creating a music development plan

In this chapter you will learn how to create a plan for the development of music across all of your departmental activities.

What is a development plan?

A development plan is a working document that helps you to improve all aspects of your music offer over time. For schools in England, prior to the release of the updated National Plan for Music Education in 2022, these were more usually known as subject action plans. The terminology may have changed, but the concept and function has not. This document will help you to keep track of all your ideas and ensure that your curriculum and co-curricular offer is consistently improving.

Defining your vision: Where do you want to be?

Chapter 2 discussed the importance of establishing your vision for music as the basis for everything that you do, and that includes your music development plan. Your vision should be the cornerstone of your plan, and everything in your plan should flow towards achieving your vision over time. If you find yourself adding actions to your plan that don't relate to your overall vision, that is an indication that something has gone wrong somewhere. Begin your plan with your vision statement and keep that in mind as you complete the remaining sections.

Here is an example vision statement:

>  **Our vision**
> Our vision for music in our school is that all students will leave us feeling that they are musical, and be equipped with the skills they need so they can engage with music in whatever way they wish in the future.

Auditing your provision: Where are you now?

In order to understand how far away you currently are from your vision, you'll need to establish where you are now. This will involve some kind of audit of your current provision.

You are likely to want to:

- identify staff development priorities (see Chapter 5)
- find out how students feel about your current music offer
- consider how students are achieving across the curriculum
- check whether your curriculum meets current statutory requirements
- identify whether you are meeting whole-school improvement goals
- look at whether you are sufficiently resourced to deliver your planned activities.

You can use any methods you like to compile the information that you need, which might include staff and student surveys or focus groups, assessment scrutiny, examination of instruments and equipment, and comparison of your curriculum documentation with the national curriculum of your country and your school's improvement plan. This will help you to build up a picture of whether you are currently achieving your vision for music, and where improvements and developments need to be made.

Here is an example conclusion that might be reached from an audit of provision:

> ### Conclusion
> Some of our students feel that the music curriculum is not for them, and that they are not learning relevant skills to pursue their own musical ambitions. As a result, options numbers at Key Stage 4 are low, and ensembles are struggling to recruit across Key Stage 3. Students would like to study contemporary genres that are relevant to them, but staff lack confidence and expertise in these areas.

Creating the detail: How do you get there?

Once you know how far away you are from achieving your vision for music, you can make a plan to get there! A great way to do this would be through the use of SMART goals, which give you 'specific, measurable, achievable, realistic and time-related' steps for improvement. Depending on how big a gap there is between your current position and where you want to be, you might split the steps down into a set of one-, three- and five-year goals. Not everything is instantly achievable, so don't be afraid to plan for the long term.

Here is an example three-year plan for Key Stage 3:

> ### In Year 1
> We will work with students to identify three key musical genres that they would like to explore. X member of staff will be given time off their timetable to research these genres and to visit other schools that have included these in their curriculum, and the budget to access training where available.

In Year 2
We will replace one lesson for each class each term across Key Stage 3 with a one-off workshop in one of these genres, led by experts in these styles, sourced in partnership with the local music hub. This will act as a launch for new co-curricular activities based around these genres, which will run throughout the remainder of the year led by the expert from the music hub, supported by X, Y and Z members of staff as part of their professional development.

In Year 3
We will fully incorporate these three genres into our curriculum, which will then feed into the co-curricular programme. X, Y, and Z, who had supported the co-curricular activities in Year 2 will now take over running these activities from the music hub in order that budget can be reassigned to other key areas of development.

Aligning with the school improvement plan

It could be argued that the only thing the SLT is really, truly invested in is the school improvement plan (SIP). This means that if you want your development plan to be taken seriously, and to be properly financially supported, you're going to have to make it clear how it supports your school's wider priorities. Fortunately, music is a subject that probably has more research studies into transferrable skills and academic and personal benefits than any other, and while these benefits are often hotly contested, this does at least mean that there will always be a way to link music to pretty much any academic, wellbeing, or social development aim!

You should definitely include a section exploring how your plan links to the school improvement plan, and you might even consider mapping your individual SMART goals against the individual targets from the SIP, just to make it really clear that both documents are pulling in the same direction.

Aligning with non-statutory guidance

If your school is based in England, there is specific advice within the non-statutory *National Plan for Music Education* (2022) about what to include in your development plan. Fortunately this is only guidance, so you are free to choose whether to include these aspects or not. *You* are the expert in *your* school, so feel free to pick and choose the aspects from this non-statutory guidance that align with your own vision, and ignore the rest!

Top tip

Don't get too hung up on non-statutory guidance – if it was really important for you to implement it, they would have made it statutory! Governments change, priorities change, and jumping on every bandwagon just causes you extra work which might become irrelevant relatively quickly! It's important to keep on top of any new guidance that is released, but use your own professional judgement to decide if you want to implement its ideas in your school. You are the expert in your own local context.

Conclusion

In this book, we have covered how to identify your vision for music in your school, and how to use this to drive forward improvement and progress. We have considered the content of your curriculum and co-curricular programmes, and how these can be linked to create strong musical provision for your school. We have looked at the process of identifying your colleagues' learning needs, and supporting them on their journey to become better at teaching music. We have also looked at the resources needed to support musical activities within your school and how to ensure that these are used effectively. And we have looked at how to articulate all of this within a plan for development.

Having read this book, you may now want to take some time to reflect on what needs to be done to develop and improve music in your school, and how you are going to go about addressing this. By reading this book you have started the journey towards revitalising music in your school. Now take as much time as you need to establish your vision and turn it into a reality. It doesn't matter if it happens next week, next term, or next year. You are on your way, and that is all anyone can ask of you.